Thimbleberries®

Autumn Accents

Contents

Copyright© 2002 by Landauer Corporation
Projects Copyright© 2002 by Lynette Jensen

This book was designed, produced, and published by Landauer Books
A division of Landauer Corporation
12251 Maffitt Road, Cumming, Iowa 50061

President: Jeramy Lanigan Landauer
Vice President Sales & Marketing: James L. Knapp
Vice President Editorial: Becky Johnston
Art Director: Laurel Albright
Creative Director: Lynette Jensen
Copy Editor: M. Peg Smith
Editorial Coordinator: Kimberly O'Brien
Photography: Craig Anderson Photography
Photostyling: Lynette Jensen and Margaret Sindelar
Technical Writer: Sue Bahr
Technical Illustrator: Lisa Kirchoff

We also wish to thank the support staff of the Thimbleberries® Design Studio:
Sherry Husske, Kathy Lobeck, Virginia Brodd, Ardelle Paulson, Renae Ashwill,
Julie Jergens, Tracy Schrantz, Clarine Howe, Pearl Baysinger, Ellen Carter, Julie Borg, and Leone Rusch.

This book is printed on acid-free paper.

Printed in China 10 9 8 7 6 5 4 3 2 1

ISBN: 1-890621-39-0

Introduction

Autumn has always been my favorite
season of the year. Even before the first
twirling leaf waltzes to the ground,
I've been busy transforming my house
and garden into a veritable cornucopia
of seasonal scent, color, texture,
and sentiment. I hope that my ideas
for using simple materials—
from candles and collectibles to pictures
and pillows—will inspire you.
Celebrate this season of plenty
with a feast of colorful autumn accents
in every nook and cranny
of your home and garden.

Wishing you the special
pleasures of autumn,

My Best,

Lynette Jensen

September Morning

September ushers in autumn with the crisp scent of cool mornings that warm to sunny afternoons—just right for gathering nature's abundant harvest.

September & Morning

When nature's brilliant *hues of
orange, red, and gold* first appear, greet
autumn at the door with a wreath hung
at the roof and generous grapevine
garlands wrapped around porch pillars.

September Morning

An iron plant cage *serves as a basket for pumpkins and gourds—
a unique way to display pumpkins that dramatically
complement evergreens, foliage, and fall flowers.*

September Morning

This wire-wheeled milk-can *frames a colorful seasonal display. The willow chair is a weathered backdrop for garden produce—from pumpkins to pinecones.*

When we remodeled *our 1930's home several years ago, we saved several shutters and a door that now grace the garden house and mirror the main house. A trio of brackets was revived and put to good use holding the window box shelf!*

September Morning

Inside the garden house, *there is a constant parade of fall flowers drying on racks and in containers of many shapes and sizes. Keeping an eclectic mix of quilts and collectibles handy allows for quick additions to autumn displays.*

September Morning

Add interest to the fall garden *by scattering simple surprises along the way. Intersperse pumpkins with interesting ceramic pottery. Give new life to a broken-bottom willow basket by letting Black-eyed Susans grow through it.*

September Morning

Keeping a large wooden bowl *close at hand makes it easy to capture the beauty of the last rose of summer. Blend rose petals with dry leaves and prop a single hydrangea blossom atop the mix for a vibrant potpourri.*

September Morning

The change of seasons is welcome *because it means bringing in the outdoors with gatherings from my garden. For containers, use everything from buckets to baskets—to brim with bountiful bouquets.*

September & Morning

For rustic tabletop displays, *decoupage vintage postcards on tins, and fill the tins with coordinating dried flowers.*

September Morning

A fitting end *to a busy day of picking apples, raking leaves, or cheering on the team at a football game—an inviting chair and a favorite quilt.*

October Gold

October is nature's paintbrush. Gild your doorstep with the season's intense colors—ranging from toasty brown to deep shades of goldenrod.

October Gold

Dried 'annabelle' hydrangea *heads, interspersed with yarrow, quickly and abundantly fill a natural grapevine wreath to overflowing.*

October Gold

To create a special welcome,
wheel in fall foliage by the bushels.
Oversize planters, such as the copper
washtub, accommodate an
abundance of hardy fall plantings that
will bloom late into the season.

Decorating with pumpkins—
as easy as one, two, three!

October Gold

Early in October, *a wizard's hat serves as a pleasant reminder that tricks and treats are just around the corner. Adirondack chairs provide plenty of parking space for autumn displays.*

October Gold

For sparkling warmth *on chilly autumn evenings, fill an old copper tub with water to float leaves and novelty pumpkin and apple candles.*

October Gold

A bountiful assortment *of colorful apples, squash, and pumpkins in a twig basket is a "natural" for a quick table arrangement. Nestle apple candles in potpourri to add a warm glow to the vignette.*

Small squash and petite pumpkins *are golden accents for
nearly every harvest arrangement. Assemble them with potpourri, ornamental
dried garden findings, candy, and quilts.*

October Gold

Special gifts for special people *are decorated with plaid ribbons and berry sprigs for a bit of autumn splendor.*

October Gold

Transform ordinary cupboards *into a harvest of autumn style.* Brighten *greens and browns with antique white accents, dried hydrangea blossoms and stemmed berries for texture, shiny apples for sheen, and textural quilts for comfort.*

October Gold

Framing a small quilt, *such as the Pumpkins for Sale wallhanging quilt shown above, creates a seasonal backdrop. The collectibles gracing the dining room sideboard draw colors from the fabrics—tying it all together for a festive display.*

October Gold

A variety of collected treasures
*is unified by color—the simplest design
principle of all.*

October Gold

Freely combine *abundant quantities of drieds to make casual autumn arrangements— the greater the variety of colors and textures the better!*

October Gold

Vintage Halloween decorations *are back by popular demand.*
For display dimension, showcase them on a crockery-filled shelf filled
with an assortment of whimsical orange and black accents. At right, pair
pumpkins, game boards, and tin stars to fill a long wall shelf with autumn gold.
Dress it all with a garland of vintage-inspired paper pumpkins.

Turn your home into
Halloween headquarters
with the many faces of the season!

October Gold

Add autumn accents *to a kitchen in a matter of minutes.*
Accent with pumpkin-appliquéd towels and fresh caramel apples—
a favorite autumn treat.

October Gold

Herald the onset of autumn
*by combining flavorful food with
earthy color flowers, serving pieces,
handsome plaid napkins,
and a harvest-themed table runner.*

October Gold

Pumpkins *abound in displays throughout the house during the autumn season. Quilts featuring pumpkins are always a favorite accessory.*

Details *are the elements that add excitement and discovery to otherwise ordinary displays. Topping off an unlidded black cookie jar with a pumpkin or squash casts an eerie shadow of candlelight against the wall.*

October Gold

For custom serving, *arrange vintage papers under the glass of an antique wooden tray. The no-bake peanut butter ghost cookies are dipped in candy coating.*

October Gold

Harvest dinners *have been a tradition since ancient Celts celebrated the gathering of newly harvested crops. Create a base for a bountiful spread by using a black-and-cream wool blanket, set with a casual mix of warm-toned decorations.*

To complement a hearty harvest supper, *select recipes that use favorite autumn ingredients. Clockwise from upper left: fresh caramel apple cake, flavorful harvest popcorn, salted peanut cookies, and creamy wild rice soup.*

October Gold

Use subtle lighting *to make Halloween magical. Candles, small lamps, and bubble lights nestled with flower arrangements and pumpkins are sure to warm every corner of the house.*

November Dusk

November is the season to be thankful for peace and plenty. Indulge in a feast of color, enhanced by the glow of candlelight, firelight, and moonlight.

November Dusk

A simple combination of apple slices topped with caramel and pecans is always a favorite autumn treat.

November Dusk

Outdoors, *a vintage corn dryer,*
strung with terra-cotta pots,
serves as a decorative accent on
the garden house wall.

November Dusk

A wire plant rack *with pots filled to overflowing with mums
and fall foliage allows just room enough for a trio of pumpkins
to make an impressive tribute to autumn.*

November Dusk

Pumpkins, pumpkins everywhere! *Pumpkins and gourds are members of the squash family, which encompass hundreds of varieties in dozens of shapes and sizes, and with such amusing names as Little Boo, Jack Be Little, and Munchkin.*

November Dusk

Jack-o'-lanterns, *displayed*
on a trellis and amid tree branches,
appear to have the last laugh
at old Jack Frost.

November Dusk

Small yet mighty—*autumn arrangements are enlivened by tucking a few sprigs of colorful berries into a harvest bouquet centerpiece or into a napkin-lined goblet. Berries contribute substance and color for naturally graceful appeal.*

November
Dusk

Stack bowls *bottom to bottom to*
create height and importance.
Nestle an apple-shape candle
in the bowl perched atop.

November Dusk

Warm wood tones *used in the framed collectibles unify this wall grouping, which includes a schoolhouse-style clock, a vintage magazine cover, a still life, and an antique turkey print. Nestling candles into dried flowers and berries adds sparkle to any setting.*

November Dusk

A densely woven market basket *anchors the assortment of autumn-hued contents that will last for weeks. Bright golden yarrow blossoms highlight the fall foliage, clusters of subtly colored berries, and rich shades of spiky dried flowers.*

November Dusk

Enhance a dried floral *arrangement by grouping such soft, textural accents as quilts and handmade rugs with colorful autumn objects.*

November Dusk

Feel free to mix and match. *Simply combine a medley of sizes, shapes, and colors that work together to create charming country-style themes.*

November Dusk

In autumn, *count on a full harvest of homegrown hydrangeas to contribute hue, texture, and volume to dried floral arrangements. For greater impact, group arrangements in multiples of three.*

November
Dusk

Painting *the walls, windows, and woodwork in rich shades of cream makes it easy to transform a room with seasonal colors.*

November Dusk

Gradually transition your decorating from season to season.
For autumn, use easy-to-acquire accents, such as harvest pumpkins,
dried florals, and an abundant mantel swag.

November Dusk

Establish family traditions *with favorite dishes, foods, and accessories.*

NovemberDusk

A study in serenity—*the softly muted shades of the still life establish*
a fitting backdrop for the trio of antique Lipton teapots.

November Dusk

Showcase dishes *with striking*
motifs to use as seasonal accents.
Here, an inviting display of
dishes includes antique transferware
in a bold turkey pattern.

November Dusk

Frame *a piece of antique patchwork to showcase autumn hues. Set out taste-tempting edible accents as well—bowls of popcorn, party mix, and candy corn. Watch them disappear.*

Arrange autumn displays *on unexpected surfaces. Layer color and texture, and amass collectibles in appealing groupings that draw attention to the season.*

November
Dusk

Amber is nature's gold.
*Create an elegant harvest
table by accenting cream and sage
with glistening amber.*

NovemberDusk

Idyllic tranquility *beckons from this autumn retreat. Ruffled pillowcases, quilts, and leaf wall stencils create a welcoming atmosphere.*

About Lynette Jensen

Expressing her creativity first through designing quilts,
Lynette discovered that by designing her own line of
coordinating fabrics she could get exactly what she needed
for her growing collection of pieced patchwork.

Known and respected throughout the quilting world for her
Thimbleberries® line of fabrics, Lynette has created an
enduring collection of coordinates in a rich palette of
country colors that spans the seasons. Lynette combines traditional quilt patterns with an
appealing array of appliquéd vines, berries, and blossoms. The result is a charming blend of
blocks and borders with soft touches of color.

For Lynette, a Minnesota native and graduate of the University of Minnesota with a
degree in Home Economics, the Thimbleberries® design studio and office is a short
walk from the home she shares with her husband, Neil. The spacious studio, filled with
antiques and quilts, is a wonderfully open and bright spot from which to work
and design each day. In this creative setting, Lynette designs fabrics
and quilts, and she develops classic country decorating themes
that express her distinctive gift for harmonizing the heart of the home.